SPOTLIGHT ON AMERICAN HISTORY

The U.S.-Mexican War and Its Impact on the United States

Rosalie Gaddi

PowerKiDS press™

NEW YORK

Published in 2017 by The Rosen Publishing Group, Inc.
29 East 21st Street, New York, NY 10010

Book Design: Samantha DeMartin

Photo Credits: Cover Everett Historical/Shutterstock.com; p. 4 Transcendental Graphics/Archive Photos/ Getty Images; p. 5 https://commons.wikimedia.org/wiki/File:Louisiana1804a.jpg; p. 7 https://en.wikipedia.org/ wiki/Declaration_of_Independence_of_the_Mexican_Empire#/media/File:Generales_del_Trigarante.jpg; p. 8 MPI/Archive Photos/Getty Images; p. 9 PHAS/Universal Images Group/Getty Images; p. 10 Bardocz Peter/ Shutterstock.com; p. 11 https://en.wikipedia.org/wiki/File:Zachary_Taylor_restored_and_cropped.png; p. 12 https://commons.wikimedia.org/wiki/File:JKP.tif; p. 13 Interim Archives/ Archive Photos/Getty Images; p. 14 https://commons.wikimedia.org/wiki/File:Battle_of_Buena_Vista_Nebel.jpg; p. 15 DEA PICTURE LIBRARY/ De Agostini Picture Library/Getty Images; p. 17 DEA/G. DAGLI ORTI/De Agostini Picture Library/Getty Images; p. 18 https://commons.wikimedia.org/wiki/File:Mexican_Cession.png; p. 19 https://en.wikipedia.org/wiki/ File:TreatyOfGuadalupeHidalgoCover.jpg; p. 21 Cathy Murphy/Hulton Archive/Getty Images.

Library of Congress Cataloging-in-Publication Data

Names: Gaddi, Rosalie, author.
Title: The U.S.-Mexican War and its impact on the United States / Rosalie
  Gaddi.
Other titles: United States-Mexican War and its impact on the United States
Description: New York : PowerKids Press, 2016. | Series: Spotlight on
  American history | Includes index.
Identifiers: LCCN 2016000860 | ISBN 9781508149606 (pbk.) | ISBN 9781508149460 (library bound) | ISBN 9781499422429 (6 pack)
Subjects: LCSH: Mexican War, 1846-1848--Juvenile literature.
Classification: LCC E404 .G33 2016 | DDC 973.6/2--dc23
LC record available at http://lccn.loc.gov/2016000860

Manufactured in the United States of America

CPSIA Compliance Information: Batch #BS16PK: For further information contact Rosen Publishing, New York, New York at 1-800-237-9932.

CONTENTS

THE AMERICAN DREAM

In the mid-1800s, the United States was going through a period of great growth and change. The population of the nation grew from around 5 million Americans in 1800 to more than 23 million only 50 years later. Americans were looking to move west to own property and start large farms, which were the backbone of the American economy. While the young country started out as 13 colonies, it had since expanded west to a new frontier.

The United States acquired a great deal of land as far west as the Mississippi River as part of the Treaty of Paris of 1783, which ended the American

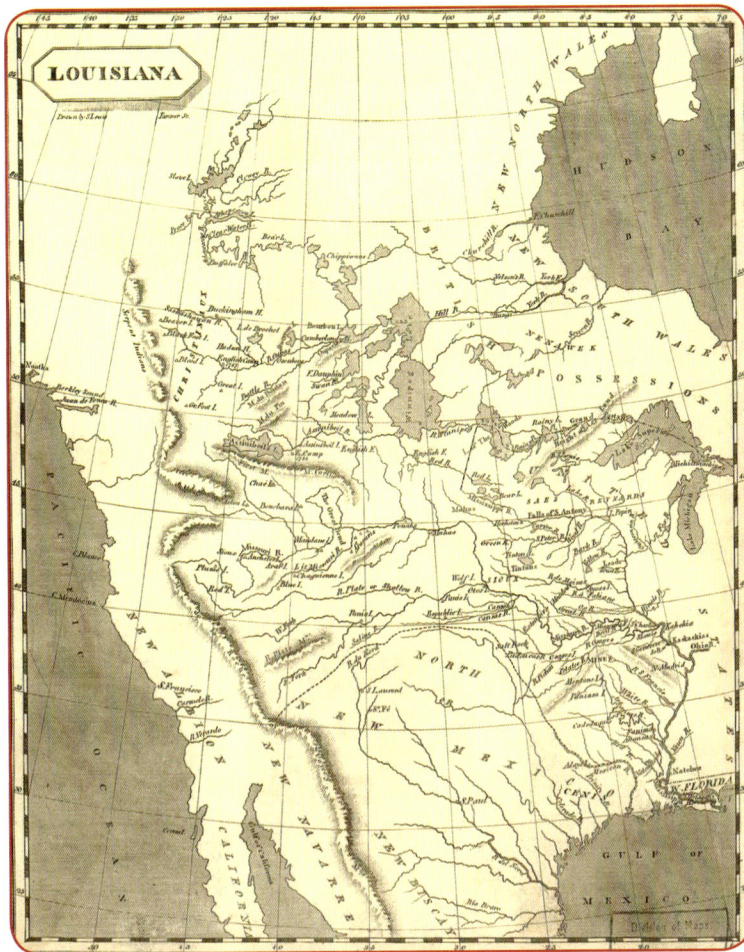

The Louisiana Purchase was an unexpected land deal for America. It opened the West up to the United States and made the American dream of westward expansion a reality.

Revolution. In 1803, President Thomas Jefferson acquired the Louisiana Territory from France through the Louisiana Purchase. This westward expansion was part of the idea of Manifest **Destiny**, or the belief that the United States should stretch across the entire continent of North America. One country that stood in the way was Mexico.

MEANWHILE, IN MEXICO

While the United States was growing and expanding, Mexico was facing hard times. It had won independence from Spain in 1821 after a war that lasted 11 years. Even though Mexico was free, it had new challenges.

Mexico faced great **debt** from the costly and long war. The new country didn't have a stable government. At first, an emperor tried to rule Mexico, but he was overthrown in 1823. A **republic** was formed and a constitution was adopted, but different political groups began fighting each other. Because the government wasn't united, Mexico suffered.

Mexico didn't have wealth or unity, but it did have land. It had won a great amount of territory that stretched from today's Mexico to northern California. However, few Mexicans lived on this land, partly because the Mexican government couldn't protect its people from native peoples living there. Those Mexicans who did move north formed their own societies that often opposed the Mexican government's rules.

The Mexican War of Independence ended with the Treaty of Córdoba, which gave Mexico its freedom and claim to the Spanish territories in the North American West. This artwork shows the Army of the Three Guarantees, the Mexican army that continued to fight Spanish forces after Mexico gained independence.

U.S. ANNEXATION OF TEXAS

Texas declared independence from Mexico on March 2, 1836, during a revolution against the Mexican government. Texans included many people of European **descent** and Tejanos, who were of Mexican and native descent. Texan forces overtook San Antonio in December 1835 and two months later, made their stand at the Alamo, a former Spanish mission. Many Texans died as Mexican forces stormed the mission. Despite the crushing loss, "Remember the Alamo" became the battle cry that helped Texas win the war, and its independence, on April 21, 1836.

Mexico threatened to attack if the United States annexed Texas. It was a risky move, but Polk went ahead with the annexation anyway.

After over a decade of difficulties with Mexico, Texas wanted to join the United States. However, the nation decided not to **annex** Texas at first. People in the North didn't want another slave state to be added to the union. In 1844, James K. Polk was elected as president of the United States. He had a strong belief that the United States should stretch across the continent. He wanted to take control of today's U.S. Southwest, as well as Texas and Oregon Country. In 1845, Texas was officially annexed by the United States.

BORDER DISPUTES

Almost immediately after the annexation of Texas, border **disputes** occurred between Mexico and the United States. While the United States believed the Texas border with Mexico was the Rio Grande, Mexico believed it was the Nueces River. Polk's continued interest in the West only increased the **tension** between the two nations.

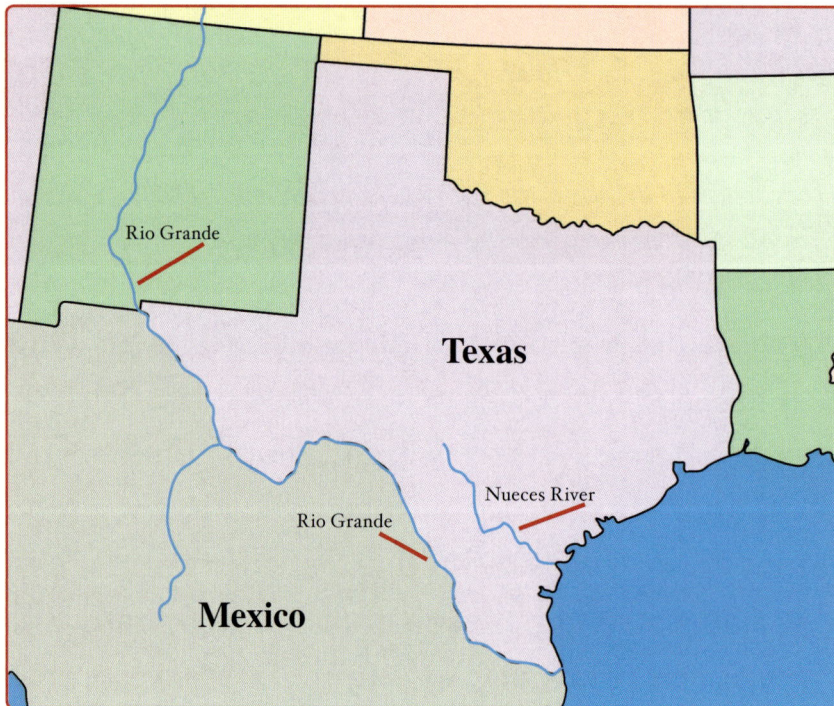

President Polk didn't want to stop at the annexation of Texas. He wanted to obtain land all the way to the Pacific Ocean. Today, the territory Polk wanted is the U.S. Southwest, including New Mexico and California.

Polk sent a U.S. **diplomat** named John Slidell to Mexico City to make a deal with the Mexican government. The United States was willing to pay up to $30 million for the Southwest territory. However, the Mexican president wouldn't negotiate. Polk

General Zachary Taylor became an American hero for his bravery and leadership in the U.S.-Mexican War. In 1849, he became the president of the United States.

ordered General Zachary Taylor to lead troops to the land between the Nueces River and Rio Grande. The land was partly in Coahuila, which was part of the former Mexican state of Coahuila y Tejas before Texas won its independence.

BLOODSHED AT THE BORDER

At this time, Mexico didn't have a very strong military or central government. It wasn't prepared to go to war. However, on April 25, 1846, Mexican **cavalry** attacked General Taylor's soldiers. They killed more than 10 men before attacking an American fort.

Other U.S. soldiers came to fight, bringing advanced weapons to beat the Mexican forces. On May 11, 1846, James Polk addressed Congress and called for war. He said Mexico had invaded American land and hurt American people. Two days later, the U.S.-Mexican War began.

James Polk

In Polk's address to Congress, he said Mexico "has passed the boundary of the United States, has invaded our territory, and shed American blood upon the American soil." This artwork shows the Battle of Resaca de la Palma, one of the first conflicts of the war.

Polk's declaration of war wasn't popular among all Americans. The United States was split into political parties. U.S. Democrats thought the war was a good idea, while Whigs thought the war was unjust. Abolitionists, or people fighting against slavery, feared new territory acquired in a war could be added to the country as slave states. Americans were divided on the issue, but whether they agreed or not, they were officially at war with Mexico.

THE WAR BEGINS

Polk sent Colonel Stephen Kearny and Commodore Robert Stockton to the Mexican territory north of the Rio Grande. They were sent to conquer the territory and take control of the land from Mexicans living there. Once they arrived, they found the few Mexicans who lived in the northern territories didn't put up much of a fight. Many of the Mexicans living in those territories had little loyalty to the Mexican government.

Battle of Buena Vista

*Mexico called upon General Antonio López de Santa Anna, a military leader who had been **exiled** to Cuba. Santa Anna told President Polk that if he were set free from his exile, he'd convince Mexico to end the war. However, after leaving Cuba, Santa Anna instead took control of the Mexican army.*

General Taylor's army was sent to conquer the city of Monterrey. In February 1847, Taylor's forces won the Battle of Buena Vista near Monterrey. His 5,000 men defeated about 15,000 Mexican troops. However, Mexico wasn't ready to back down yet.

Polk wanted to launch a major invasion of Mexico by sea, but General Taylor was against it. Polk found another general up to the fight—General Winfield Scott.

A STRING OF VICTORIES

Because Mexico still wouldn't surrender, Polk sent General Scott to attack Mexico by sea. Scott's forces led a nearly three-week siege against Veracruz, which was an important seaport with a fort. On March 9, 1847, 10,000 American soldiers landed on a beach near Veracruz to begin the siege. They trapped nearly 3,000 Mexican troops inside the city and 1,000 more inside the fort. On March 28, Mexican forces surrendered their city, fort, and army to U.S. forces.

From Veracruz, Scott's forces continued on to Mexico City. They used the path that explorer and **conquistador** Hernán Cortés used when he conquered the Aztec people. They met Mexican forces along the way but had a string of victories.

Once in Mexico City, U.S. troops began a siege of Chapultepec Castle. Mexico City fell to the United States in September 1847. With this major defeat of Mexico, the fighting was finally over.

On September 13, 1847, U.S. troops stormed Chapultepec Castle. During the battle, several Mexican cadets, or military students, fought to the death instead of leaving when their general ordered a retreat. They became known as "Los Niños Héroes" or "Hero Children."

TREATY OF GUADALUPE HIDALGO

The last major battle of the U.S.-Mexican War was the fall of Mexico City. Some sources say as many as 25,000 Mexican soldiers were killed in battle during the war, compared with only 1,733 U.S. soldiers. It had been a costly war for Mexico, in both lives and resources. However, the war wasn't over. The two nations still had to agree on borders and just how much Mexico would lose after its surrender.

*The land **ceded** by Mexico to the United States was called the Mexican Cession.*

cover of the Treaty of Guadalupe Hidalgo

The Mexican government was in ruins, but it still had to make a treaty with the United States. On February 2, 1848, officials from both nations signed the Treaty of Guadalupe Hidalgo. It was then approved by both congresses.

The Treaty of Guadalupe Hidalgo gave the United States the territory that includes today's states of California, New Mexico, Utah, Nevada, Arizona, Texas, and parts of Colorado and Wyoming. In exchange, the United States agreed to pay Mexican debts against U.S. citizens. The United States also paid Mexico $15 million for the land.

POSTWAR MEXICO

When Mexico won its independence from Spain, it was a nation of possibility. It was largely in debt and its government was divided, but it had its freedom and a great amount of land. The U.S.-Mexican War was a great loss for Mexico. Not only was the war-torn country drained of resources, it was also drained of potential. Mexico had lost the land that would produce gold and become rich in agriculture under the control of the United States.

The Mexicans who had been living in the lands of the Mexican Cession had to choose between Mexican or American citizenship. When American settlers came west, they brought their own culture, or ways of life, that sometimes conflicted with Mexican culture. The former Mexicans became strangers in their own land. They clung to their culture and their strong Catholic faith, but many were treated with inequality. Many lost their land to the newcomers.

Mexican Americans continued to be treated with inequality for well over a hundred years. In the 1960s, many Mexican Americans united in the Mexican American Civil Rights Movement for equality. Many continue to fight for fair treatment today.

THE UNITED STATES PUSHES WEST

The United States also faced losses during the U.S.-Mexican War. While around 1,700 died in battle, more than 10,000 troops died of illness. Diseases such as yellow fever, smallpox, and measles spread quickly because of poor, dirty conditions.

However, the war was largely successful for the United States. The Mexican Cession added more than 500,000 square miles (1,294,994 sq km) to the nation. After the purchase of much of the Oregon Territory from Britain in 1846 and the Mexican Cession, the United States stretched from the Atlantic Ocean to the Pacific Ocean. There were still disputes over borders, but the Gadsden Purchase of 1854 extended the U.S. border even further into Mexico to create part of Arizona and New Mexico.

The Mexican Cession opened the West up for settlement. The California Gold Rush from 1848 to 1855 brought thousands of people to California looking to strike it rich. Americans who moved west held tightly to the promise of property and wealth. The U.S.-Mexican War changed more than the size of the United States—it achieved the dream of Manifest Destiny.

GLOSSARY

annex (AA-nehks): To take over an area and make it part of a larger territory.

cavalry (KAA-vuhl-ree): The part of an army made up of soldiers trained to fight on horseback.

cede (SEED): To give control of something to another person or government.

conquistador (kahn-KEE-stuh-dohr): A Spanish conqueror or adventurer.

debt (DEHT): An amount of money owed to someone or something.

descent (duh-SEHNT): Coming from a certain background.

destiny (DEHS-tuh-nee): The things that are meant to happen in the future.

diplomat (DIH-ploh-mat): A person who is skilled at talks between nations.

dispute (dihs-PYOOT): To argue about something.

exile (EHK-syl): A situation in which someone is forced to leave their country to live in another place.

republic (rih-PUH-blik): A country that's governed by elected representatives and an elected leader.

tension (TEN-chuhn): A state of unrest between individuals or groups.

INDEX

PRIMARY SOURCE LIST

Cover: *The Storming of Chapultepec.* Chromolithograph. Distributed by Nathaniel Currier in 1848. Lithograph created by Sarony & Major based on a painting by "Walker." Now kept at the National Museum of American History, Washington, D.C.

Page 12: Portrait of James Knox Polk. Photograph. Created by Mathew Brady. Circa 1845 to 1849. Now kept at the Library of Congress Prints and Photographs Division, Washington, D.C.

Page 14: *Battle of Buena Vista.* Lithograph by Adolphe Jean-Baptiste Bayot based on a drawing by Carl Nebel. Published in book *The War Between the United States and Mexico, Illustrated* in 1851 in New York, NY. Now kept at the University of Texas at Arlington Library, Arlington, TX.

WEBSITES

Due to the changing nature of Internet links, PowerKids Press has developed an online list of websites related to the subject of this book. This site is updated regularly. Please use this link to access the list: www.powerkidslinks.com/soah/usmex